THIS BOOK BELONGS TO:

Cambridge English
Young Learners

A–Z Colouring Book

You can use this colouring book to help children learn new words in a fun way and improve their English. It includes many of the words children might see in their test.

The words have been selected from the *Cambridge English: Young Learners* Word List. They cover all three levels: *Starters*, *Movers* and *Flyers*.

For more free support materials visit:

Aa

alien

Bb

boat

Cc

castle

Dd

dinosaur

Ee

elephant

Ff

fish

Gg

guitar

Hh

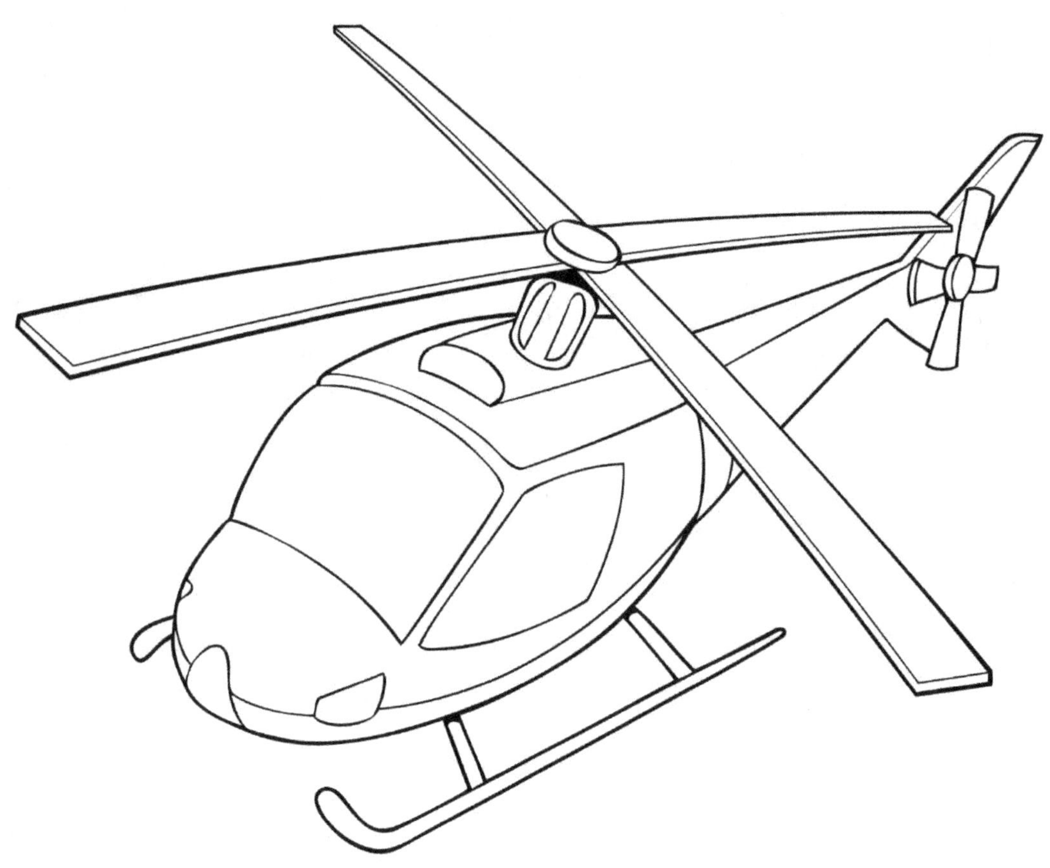

helicopter

Ii

insect

Jj

jungle

Kk

kangaroo

Ll

lion

Mm

monkey

Nn

nurse

Oo

octopus

Pp

parrot

Qq

queen

Rr

rocket

Ss

spider

Tt

train

Uu

umbrella

Vv

violin

Ww

whale

Xx

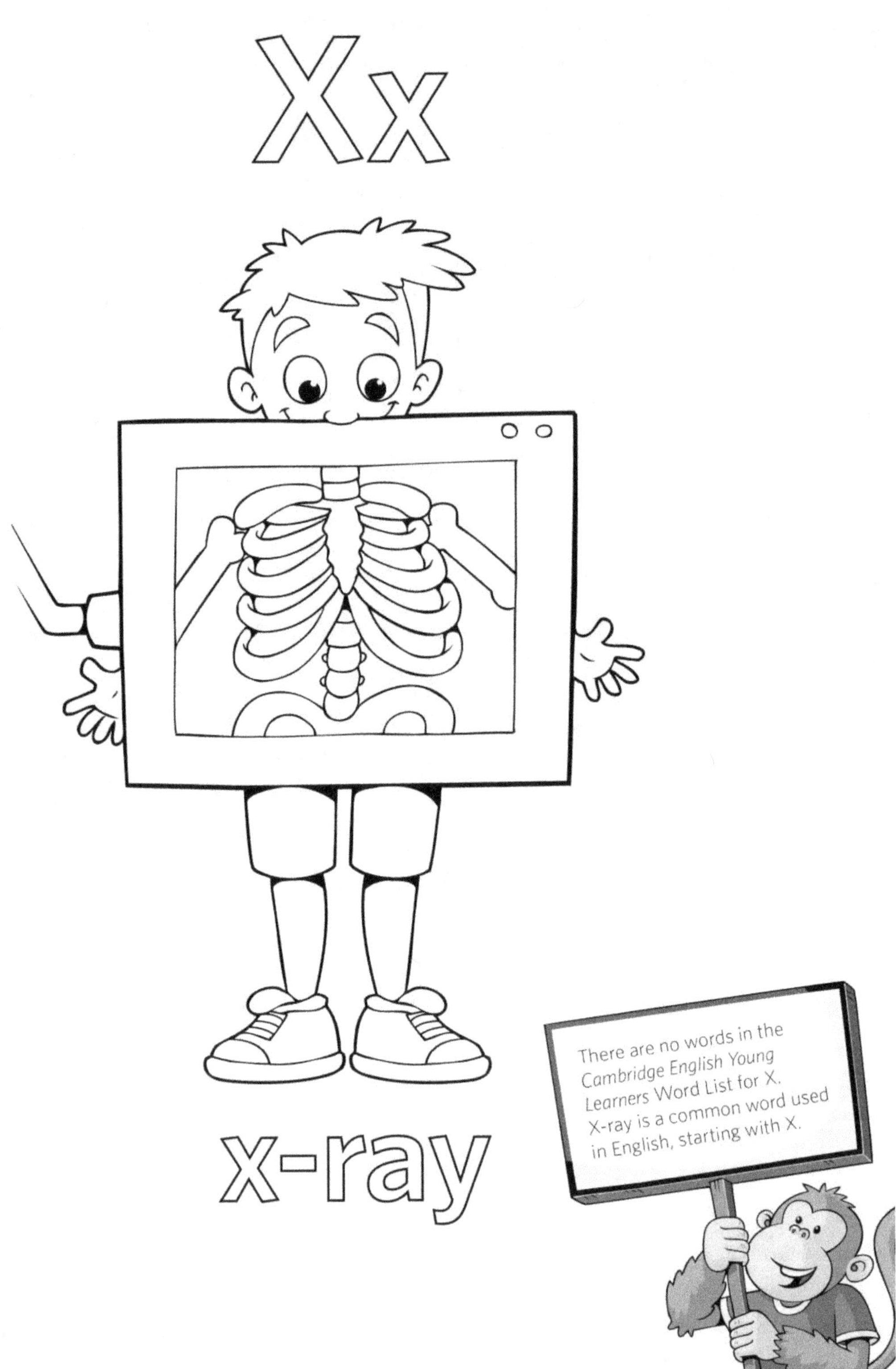

x-ray

There are no words in the
Cambridge English Young
Learners Word List for X.
X-ray is a common word used
in English, starting with X.

Yy

young

Zz

ZOO

I hope you like it